Wellness Creation

A WORKBOOK AND JOURNAL TO GUIDE YOUR WELLNESS JOURNEY

Dr. Robert L. Wilson Jr., DSL

ARCHWAY
PUBLISHING

Archway Publishing books may be ordered through booksellers or by contacting:

Archway Publishing
1663 Liberty Drive
Bloomington, IN 47403
www.archwaypublishing.com
844-669-3957

ISBN: 978-1-6657-4577-2 (sc)
ISBN: 978-1-6657-4578-9 (e)

Print information available on the last page.

Archway Publishing rev. date: 08/07/2023

I would like to acknowledge, thank, and dedicate this workbook and journal to all the people who want to live well and successfully—to those who dare to discover, unlock, and maximize their potential and possibilities for optimal wellness, and to those who are willing to do the work and tap into their power to create the life and wellness they want. Much success on your journey!

Contents

Contents

Preface

This workbook was created with you in mind. It was developed to help you become aware, understand, and apply this information about wellness creation to get unstuck, get clarity, gain momentum, develop discipline, and tap into your self-determination and motivation for optimal success. The workbook provides you with the tools, strategies, and the process necessary for you to take inspired action to create, change, improve, and get the results and outcomes you want! If this resonates with you, then stay tuned to what is coming up next during the rest of this journey.

I hope that this workbook and journal will help you to raise your awareness and build literacy toward increasing your wellness from the inside out. I would like to dispel the myth that change starts on the outside. The goal is not merely to change your behavior in order to change your outcomes or results, but to empower you with understanding and making the choices that will bring the results you desire. Your behaviors reflect your self-image of what wellness is and how it applies to you—what it looks, sounds, and feels like for you internally. Your behavior will support outwardly what's happening inwardly. You can choose a new behavior, but first you must choose your self-image, which will be supported or reflected in your behavior. The image that you see, the vision of your wellness, is the missing component of how to create lasting change and true transformation (Wilson 2023, viii).

I created this workbook to help you to do the inner work necessary to create your desired wellness. The inner work is not trying or forcing change but relaxing and allowing the process to work with and for you as you learn about yourself and how to apply this information for your success. The work starts by understanding the concepts of wellness as a foundational tool of knowledge. Next you have an opportunity to do the work by applying what you learned to your situation for yourself. You are provided the space and time to acquire this knowledge and create strategies intentionally in a way that is intimate and unique to you, so that you may better understand how this information can be used effectively and successfully for your desired level of wellness and overall quality of life. When you take inspired action in applying and practicing the information, true learning and transformation occur. A workbook should not just be about completing exercises and finishing the book; the goal is to guide you in *how* you process the information, tap into your motivation and determination, and transfer the learning into other areas for your success.

The concepts are shared first, then opportunities for both application and practice are provided. This process is based on a method of education that includes development and training components for a richer and more robust learning experience. The information in this book is not a how-to prescription but rather a foundation for both inductive and deductive learning opportunities. I am sharing principles and a process that is deductive, while the questions, activities, reflection, application, and practice of the content is inductive (INLP Center website). The principles and information are not for reading only but for putting these principles into practice and action consistently and persistently to maximize your results (Hill, 2017, p.130).

I present this opportunity and space for you to take a deep dive into *you*. This is a guided journey that lays the foundation for real transformative and lasting work that will help you to shift and become empowered to live the life you truly want. Wellness is about finding your true self and tapping into the unlimited reservoir and potential that is within you. Wellness starts from the inside out. You have the power within you to create, attract, produce, and experience the life and wellness that you so desire (Dyer 1997, xi).

In part 1, each chapter shares the application of the concept to help reinforce your understanding and to provide you with opportunities to practice, increasing your competence and confidence in how to increase your wellness dimensionally and holistically. This infrastructure is used to assist readers like you with successfully navigating, creating, and improving their wellness. You will be connecting your self-image of wellness to *affirmations*, statements that positively affirm, and to *afformations* in question form, which positively engage your mind in finding reasons to support an answer to the question you posed. This two-sided process will help reprogram your behaviors from the inside out and reinforce the wellness self-image that you want to address and redefine.

In part 2, you set off on your journey, putting the concepts, principles, and information into practice. It is all about your reflection, application, insight, awareness, determination, motivation, learning, and practice as you walk into your destiny. You will get to see the changes, growth, development, and progress as you embark on this thirty-day journey, which you will capture by writing down your experience. You were born to create! Now release your power to do so through wellness creation.

Dr. Robert L. Wilson Jr., DSL

Introduction: Wellness

The National Wellness Institute defines wellness as "a process of becoming aware of making choices toward a more successful existence." I offer this definition because when you understand that wellness is more than eating right and exercising, you are ready to learn that wellness is also about your awareness of the power of choice and how you use that awareness to create a more successful life. Through this workbook, you will learn that there are in fact eight dimensions of wellness that impact your overall quality of life. Understanding these eight dimensions will help you on your journey by creating strategic wellness goals and plans for each of these dimensions. Considering how you define wellness and what it will look, feel, or sound like for you will help you to expand your view or perspective more holistically. These eight dimensions have been adapted from the Substance Abuse and Mental Health Services Administration (SAMHSA) in conjunction with other concepts to guide you on your wellness creation journey.

Part 1 approaches the creation of wellness as the choice, commitment, and responsibility of the individual (Arloski 2014, 39). The workbook challenges and provides you with opportunities to raise your awareness of what these choices, commitments, and responsibilities look like for you. The power of choice is a game changer for you. Why? Because you have the power and ability to choose wellness intentionally and not just let it happen accidentally. This new awareness and insight will then empower you to apply and practice the knowledge in creating the level of wellness you desire. My "Robert Wilsonism" on this is that people can't be empowered until they first recognize that they have power. You have the power of choice! What will you choose?

It is critical to your success to realize that you have the ability, choices, and power to change things for yourself. Let me say that again: you have the ability, choices, and power to change things for yourself! This is not about telling you what to do or how to do it; it's about bringing an awareness of the information, process, application, and practice to you so that you can shift your quality of life and overall wellness for yourself intentionally and strategically. It is important that you feel that you *can* do this; if you do, you will understand how to create a new level of wellness by developing new thoughts and feelings that will produce new actions (Schneider 2022, 189). I am here on this journey with you to encourage you to believe in yourself and your ability to create the life and wellness that you truly want and deserve.

Now let's talk about the eight dimensions of wellness that offer a model for you in defining and redefining your wellness goals. These are:

1. **spiritual wellness**, finding spiritual fulfillment, purpose, meaning, and knowing your true identity (can include but not necessarily religious);
2. **intellectual wellness**, using mental and intellectual capabilities to create, expand, and think in healthy ways;
3. **emotional wellness**, the awareness, recognition, and ability to make positive shifts emotionally;
4. **financial wellness**, financial literacy, awareness, wealth, and freedom;
5. **physical wellness**, exercise, activity, health, nutrition, and fitness;
6. **social wellness,** healthy, happy, fulfilling relationships and interactions
7. **occupational wellness**, work that brings skills, satisfaction, expansion, empowerment, fulfillment, and purpose
8. **environmental wellness**, physical and mental environments conducive to providing safety, support, and stimulation.

These definitions of the eight dimensions provide a baseline as you explore, study, and define what each looks, feels, and sounds like in regard to *your* wellness. For additional information on the eight dimensions of wellness, the wellness initiative, and other resources, go to the SAMHSA website at https://store.samhsa.gov/product/What-You-Need-to-Know-About-National-Wellness-Week/sma16-4952.

This workbook and journal take the model of the eight dimensions and builds upon the concepts using self-image, affirmations, and afformations to guide you in processing and applying the information for your wellness creation to live the life you desire.

Part 1 offers a broad view of wellness to assist with raising your awareness to the concept of wellness so that you can decide more specifically how wellness is defined for you. The purpose is to empower you to set wellness goals and move toward them. This section will assist you in understanding your current mind-*set* and how to move towards a mind-*shift*, empowering and educating yourself by making a positive connection between your self-image and the dimensions of wellness (Arloski 2014, xxiii). In part 1, you will be expanding your capacity and ability to make positive changes toward wellness. First, let's outline some concepts.

Self-Image

Self-image is your internal view or image of yourself, constructed from your thoughts, experiences, and the words you use, or the words used toward you by others. Your self-image influences how you see yourself and how wellness looks, feels, and sounds to you (Wilson 2023, 5). For instance, when I say "wellness," what do you think of? Someone exercising and eating healthily? Or someone who is financially fit, enjoying work in a chosen career, or who has socially fulfilling relationships? All of those are within the scope of the eight dimensions of wellness. Are they in your scope of wellness and how do you see yourself?

Your wellness is an external mirror of what you have developed and believed on the inside, reflected from your self-image. Changing your behaviors to live a healthier life without changing your internal paradigm or self-image would be difficult. Building a healthier lifestyle starts with how you view yourself and the process of creating a well-life vision from the inside out (Arloski 2014, 157). How do you construct a self-image? By mentally painting a clear picture of what you desire in your imagination. Then hold that image with your will repetitiously and consistently until the image takes root, grows, and is formed inside, then manifests outwardly (Hill 2017, 132).

Self-Awareness and Self-Determination

Self-awareness is your ability to intentionally and consciously recognize aspects of the eight dimensions that contribute to your wellness. *Self-determination* is your ability to use your will intentionally and consciously to focus and change the factors that contribute to your wellness choices. Wellness behaviors reflect your level of self-awareness and self-determination in connection with your self-image. So, it's important to raise your awareness of what wellness is and to actively shape how you see the challenges or opportunities to improve it. Your determination and motivation will work in conjunction with your awareness as you apply the information you have gathered to your individual wellness goals, strategies, and plan.

Both awareness and determination are self-governed. That means the choice is yours! You have the power to choose. Making your own wellness choices means that you are fully engaged in the process on your wellness journey. By understanding self-determination, you can become more conscious and directed, enhancing your motivation to reach your desired goal of wellness. Self-awareness and self-determination must be connected by intentional organized thinking, which consists of persistent action and application of these principles in your life practices, leading to development, growth, and transformation in your overall wellness (Hill 2017, 130).

Self-awareness and self-determination are key ingredients for creating strategies, goals, and plans that reflect your willingness and capacity for change. Setting goals is not about being told what to do—it's about tapping into your own readiness for change (Arloski 2014, 166–167). True change starts with raising your awareness and assessing your level of determination to effectively set goals and implement strategies for your wellness creation success.

Self-Determination Theory

Self-determination theory is a broad framework for understanding factors that contribute to both determination and motivation for wellness (Ryan and Deci, 2020, 1). Internal or intrinsic motivation is what motivates you from within or internally influences your behavior; for example, a sense of pride, accomplishment, achievement, or progress toward a goal or outcome. External or extrinsic motivation comes from the outside or external perceptions that influence behavior; for example, trying to lose weight, or wanting a new wardrobe, new or more fulfilling relationships, more money, a better job, or a new home. Your internal and external motivations combine to form your capacity for and expression of your self-determination.

Because motivation is shaped by "the distinctions between intrinsic and extrinsic goals and their impact on motivation and wellness," as described by the Center for Self-Determination, it is important to become aware of both your intrinsic and extrinsic motivations to better understand what motivates you from the inside out. This awareness leads to gaining knowledge of self—the knowledge of *you*. Knowledge of your self-image as it relates to wellness dimensionally along with the ability to govern and choose to improve your wellness—that is, exercising your autonomy—will take you to the level of competence and self-determination you need to make the necessary changes and to succeed (Martela and Ryan 2015, 2). This journey is within you. The starting point for your determination is based on the definiteness of your desire and the strength of your motivation consistently infused with your emotional charge, which is facilitated by your motivation to lock in and bring it to pass (Hill 2017, 132). In other words, your determination and motivation are a team that works and is fueled most effectively when combined with your positive emotional energy, such as excitement and enthusiasm, to obtain what you really want!

The aim of the self-determination theory is to help individuals like you to take self-responsibility, self-accountability, and self-empowerment. Self-determination is about not placing the blame on other people, circumstances, or external factors. By gaining a better understanding of not only the journey to wellness but the journey through yourself, you can reach your goals more effectively. You determine your outcome and results! Again, you determine your outcome and results!

Transfer of Learning Theory

Now that you are determined to create the level of wellness that you want, how does learning transfer? Transfer of learning theory is based on the idea that knowledge learned in a particular area can be used and applied in other areas. This theory helps to ensure that you can apply or transfer the knowledge acquired in this workbook under different circumstances and in various ways that benefit you in reaching your goals (Hajian 2019, 94). Why is this important to you? By raising your awareness, you become engaged in your learning process, locating opportunities for applying the content and implementing these intentions and strategies into your life practices. You leave with the information and the tools to create wellness in any of the eight dimensions that we will be covering in the workbook. Once you get the tools, the workbook guides you on when, where, why, and how to use them to get the results and success that you want.

The aim of this theory is to help you not only to use what you are learning while you are going through the workbook but to continue using it and applying it throughout your life for continued success, transformation, and empowerment. Many people are not aware of how they learn and, more importantly, how to use what they have learned in other ways that benefit them. This theory helps you to understand that you are also learning about yourself and how you digest the information you are receiving. Review this information as many times as you need to—this workbook and journal are constructed for you to continue to use repeatedly. Each time you will gain new insight, awareness, and revelation for yourself and your journey.

Study and Practice

Information and tools to create wellness will benefit you only as much as you decide to study, understand, and use them. "The only way to develop understanding is through study" (Proctor, 2021, 129), which will lead to transformation, change, and the results that you desire. The self-education component needed for true change means effectively demonstrating the application and study of the information consistently can and will produce practices that foster greater wellness results for you (Wilson 2023, 19). Your determination, motivation, transfer of learning, and study will make the difference and be the difference in your wellness results and outcomes.

You are studying yourself just as much as you are studying the information. Study is both intentional and strategic. Self-discipline and organized thinking are needed to choose the thought habits that will allow you to study and practice, using the information to reach your goal and attain what you truly desire (Hill 2017, 146). This workbook is designed for you to take your time to reflect, digest, and think about the information and how it can be used effectively by you in real life. Self-image, mind-set, and mind-shift are important to study and practice for a successful wellness journey.

Self-Image, Mind-Set, and Mind-Shift

Mind-set and mind-shift play an important role in creating your self-image of wellness, and they are instrumental in navigating your journey effectively.

You often hear that mind-set is everything, but what does that mean? What is the importance of identifying and changing your mind-set when it comes to your wellness? If you recognize that your mind-set needs to change, how can you shift it? Your self-image reflects your mind-set. Mind-sets are fixed ways of thinking and beliefs that have created your current self-image. To change your self-image or create a new one, there must be a mind-shift, which will move you from your current way of thinking to a new way of thinking or believing that will produce a different image. It is important to understand your mind-set to get your mind working for and not against you.

It is critical to your wellness and empowerment to understand that your self-image reflects your beliefs and ways of thinking that influence your behavior and results (Gomas 2017). A mind-shift means first identifying the current image along with those past or current fixed beliefs that are no longer serving you, and then replacing those beliefs with new beliefs that support the new image and the results you want to create. Wellness is a result of understanding the connection of your self-image to your mind-set and how to make a mind-shift from your current level of wellness to your new desired level of wellness. Your wellness results and outcomes relate to how you think and your understanding of how to positively shift your mind-set from the negative impact of those results and outcomes. This workbook is designed to help you to identify and locate your current mind-set and the mind-shift that is needed to help you to create the level of wellness you desire—what you want to be, do, and have in the eight dimensions of wellness.

The Power of Words: Affirmations and Afformations

Your words are very powerful in helping with your mind-shift for wellness. Words help in creating your image and your wellness. Your words reinforce your degree and level of wellness, as well as help produce your outcomes and results: "Your words become a powerful indicator of your beliefs and results" (Wilson 2023, 12).

I will discuss two ways to use your words positively and strategically: *affirmations* and *afformations*. Affirmations are powerful, positive, present-tense statements; afformations are powerful, positive, present-tense questions that encourage you to develop your mind-set and belief system, providing strategies and insights for creating a new or desired image from within.

The concepts I've been covering in this introduction are essential to understand and apply as you work through the topics in this workbook and put them into practice to form a strategic plan. Everything is interconnected and interrelated.

Part 1 of this workbook will help you to understand concepts, raise your awareness, discuss application, and provide you the opportunity to practice the information shared. Part 2 will give you the opportunity to reflect on the information shared and discover how you can use it on your wellness journey dimensionally and holistically.

PART 1

Wellness Creation Workbook

1

Setting Expectations

Let's begin by establishing some objectives. In the workbook, we will

- define and discuss wellness from a dimensional yet holistic perspective;
- identify and demonstrate the role of self-image, feelings, and behavior in wellness;
- discuss the role of self-awareness and self-determination in wellness;
- explain how the theory of self-determination can be applied strategically to enhance your motivation for creating and increasing wellness.

First, recognize that you have the power and the ability to empower yourself by setting expectations in your own words. This is an important aspect of creating the level of wellness you desire. The following questions will help you assess where you are on your journey.

1. Based on what you've learned so far, what do you see as the purpose of this workbook for you? Do you have wellness goals? What changes or improvements would you like to create in your life? What do you want to be, do, or have? What does it look, feel, or sound like?

2. How did you define wellness before beginning this workbook?

3. How does the introduction to this book define wellness? How does this help you with your definition of wellness? Are any of these concepts about wellness new to you? What are your new insights? New awareness? New thoughts?

4. How would you define wellness now? Be descriptive and detailed. What does it look, feel, or sound like?

5. What do you hope to gain from reading and doing the inner work provided by this workbook? How might this workbook help you on your wellness journey?

2

The Eight Dimensions

This lesson is both our starting point and the framework of this workbook. The eight dimensions of wellness will be the model you build your wellness on. These concepts will be your blueprint to what wellness consists of dimensionally and holistically. It will serve as your foundation to build the life you want.

The eight dimensions allow you to define wellness in a way that is digestible and can be put into practice easily and efficiently to yield the best results for you. This approach provides an easy way to see the connection among the dimensions and how they can be used to identify and implement wellness goals and strategies intentionally and effectively.

Without looking back at the definitions given in the introduction, how would you define and describe each of the eight dimensions in your own words? This is to help you to start capturing the essence, image, and words of what wellness will look, feel, or sound like for you. Your level and degree of wellness will depend on how you create and define what it is for you.

1. Spiritual

2. Intellectual

3. Emotional

4. Financial

5. Physical

6. Social

7. Occupational

8. Environmental

Now please take some time to pause and review the eight dimensions as presented in the introduction to this book. Feel free to expand or revise any of your answers from above as you reflect on each dimension as it relates to your goals and desires for wellness creation. It is important that you start to think about and notice how you want your wellness creation to look, feel, and sound so that you can develop the image of wellness in each dimension for yourself.

Dr. Robert L. Wilson Jr., DSL

Activity: Expectations

5 minutes

Choose one of the eight dimensions of wellness that you would like to improve, change, or create a new image for. Take five minutes to write about why.

Based on my experience, what's most useful is for you to think about what that dimension currently looks, feels, or sounds like and then what you really *want*, not just what you think you can have. There's a difference. This is about you and what you want, so give yourself permission to dream big here and let go of your fears and inhibitions.

Continue to focus on this dimension of wellness as you work through chapters 3–9. You may repeat these chapters to cover all eight dimensions of wellness later to review any dimension you feel is needed. At the end of part 1, space is provided for you to reflect on each of the eight dimensions as you intentionally form your strategic wellness plan.

3

Self-Image

In this section, we'll be exploring your self-image concerning the dimension of wellness that you want to change, improve, or create a new image for, which you identified in the previous activity.

Self-image is the starting point of your wellness journey. This journey starts on the inside. We will begin to navigate the inner image you have of yourself. Remember, your self-image is the internal picture or image you see or visualize of yourself within the dimension of wellness that you are choosing to focus on right now. It is important to realize that you have a self-image or internal picture already established. The goal here is to empower you by noticing and becoming aware of what the self-image is and how you can intentionally and strategically recreate it as the self-image that you want.

The following questions are guides to what the self-image will be for you.

1. What is your self-image within this dimension of wellness?

2. How is your self-image created?

Dr. Robert L. Wilson Jr., DSL

3. How would you like to change or improve your self-image in this dimension?

4. What obstacles do you see to changing or improving your self-image? How can you overcome these obstacles?

Activity: Self-Image

15 minutes

Based on the answers you just provided, take fifteen minutes to define and describe your self-image within the dimension of wellness you've chosen to explore. You may draw a picture or diagram, list words that describe or define your self-image in this dimension or write a poem or story about your self-image. Your creativity and expression are welcome to assist you to best capture the image that you desire.

4

Self-Awareness and Self-Determination

This section is about gaining understanding and using opportunities to notice, be curious, and express no judgment in the process of being present and aware of your thoughts, feelings, and interactions.

Self-awareness is your ability to intentionally and consciously recognize various aspects of the eight dimensions that contribute to your wellness. Self-awareness is consciously noticing the words you use concerning the outcomes and results you get. *Self-determination* is your ability to intentionally and consciously use your will to focus on how to change aspects, components, and factors that contribute to your wellness choices. Self-determination is intentionally using your will and words in collaboration to effectively create what you want. This is about you moving from having intentions to making decisions, engaging your will to lay hold of and confirm what you want and desire.

It is important to raise your awareness by noticing your words and how they work either for or against you. Your determination or motivation allows you to transform and use the information you gain from your awareness and insight into inspired action by the way you intentionally speak from this point forward. Your wellness behaviors reflect your level of self-awareness and self-determination in connection with your self-image.

1. How would you define self-awareness? When have you used your self-awareness? Provide an example from your own experience of a moment where you felt that you made an advancement in your self-awareness within the dimension you have

chosen to explore or think of something that you would like to become more self-aware of within that dimension. The goal here is to build your noticing and awareness skills.

2. How would you define self-determination? When have you used your self-determination? Provide an example from your own experience of a moment where you felt you made an advancement in your self-determination within the dimension you have chosen to explore. The goal here is to notice and become aware of your determination.

3. What do you see as the difference between self-awareness and self-determination?

Activity: Self-Awareness and Self-Determination

15 minutes

Take fifteen minutes to explore your motivation. This will be key to becoming aware of what motivates you and how you can intentionally use it to create a strategic plan to succeed.

1. What will help motivate you to change, improve, or succeed at creating a new image in relation to the wellness dimension that you chose to explore at the end of chapter 2?

2. What is your internal motivation? What are the things within yourself that motivate or internally influence you, and how can they help to keep you motivated to accomplish your desired level of wellness?

3. What is your external motivation? What are the things outside yourself that externally motivate or influence you, and how can these help keep you motivated to accomplish your desired level of wellness?

4. How do the internal and external motivations combine to create your self-motivation? How will self-motivation help you on your wellness journey?

5

Self-Determination Theory

People must take responsibility for their lives and circumstances to be truly empowered (Gomas 2017, 216). Self-determination theory captures the essence of motivation and the need for autonomy, competence, and relatedness. *Autonomy* is your freedom to choose; *competence* is your ability or skills to do something; and *relatedness* is how things are connected for you. For example, you have the autonomy-choice or freedom to be healthy or not. You can choose different methods of how you can create the health you desire. You can choose to implement a workout routine to create the healthy lifestyle you desire. Your competence then is your ability to effectively implement the workout routine. The relatedness is you choosing to implement running because you were on your high school track team and running is something you enjoy but haven't done in years. Running relates to a time in your life where things were fun, enjoyable, and you felt good. This increases your determination and motivation to succeed and reach your goals. Your autonomy, competence, and relatedness work together to reinforce your ability through determination and motivation to produce the outcomes you desire.

The Self-determination theory can help you on your wellness journey by showing that you choose what you want your wellness to be, you can learn how to create wellness, and you can acquire the related concepts that will help you to reach your goals. The level of determination you need to create improvement and change comes from knowledge of your self-image, relatedness to your wellness dimensionally, and the ability to govern and make choices toward wellness (Martela and Ryan 2015, 2).

A major element of self-determination theory is self-education on internal and external motivational factors, as we saw in the previous chapter. Motivation helps you set and reach positive outcomes through the exercise of autonomy, competence, and relatedness (Ryan and Deci 2020, 1). Setting goals based on your own internal and external motivational factors is more beneficial than setting goals and then trying to find ways to become motivated to reach those goals. Setting goals produces the results you want when you are free to choose what those goals are, have the skills to create what you want, and understand how to connect your goals and skills to the wellness that you are creating for your success.

1. How would you define *autonomy* in relation to the wellness dimension you've chosen to explore?

2. What would give you a feeling of competence or the ability to create what you want in this wellness dimension?

3. What is relatedness or the connection that you have within the dimension you have chosen to explore?

4. List your internal motivations for improving this wellness dimension.

5. List your external motivations for improving this wellness dimension.

Dr. Robert L. Wilson Jr., DSL

6. What are your internal motivations that you can use in this dimension? What are your external motivations that you can use in this dimension? Combine them. What is your self-motivation to help you create your desire within this dimension?

Activity: Self- Determination Theory

15 minutes

Take fifteen minutes to explore your autonomy/choices, your competence/ability, and your relatedness/connection within the dimension of wellness you've chosen to focus on. What have you noticed? How can you use this for your motivation and determination?

6

Mind-Set and Mind-Shift

Creating your wellness starts with a thought. Your way of thinking, or mind-set, creates your current outcomes and results. If you would like to see different outcomes and results, you must move out of your current mind-set to a mind-shift in what you would desire. All external or physical manifestations of wellness are based on the internal thoughts you consistently and repetitiously focus on as reflected in your habits and physical actions—wellness results begin in the form of a thought in your mind (Hill 2017, 134). It is imperative to your success and wellness goals that you recognize the role, importance, and function of mind-set and mind-shift in wellness creation.

Your ability to create the wellness you desire is interdependent on being aware of your current mind-set, or the way that you think, and your mind-shift, or the way you would like to think, regarding your wellness. Mind-set and mind-shift influence and impact your determination to have what you desire.

You locate your mind-set by looking at your current results in each of the dimensions of wellness. Ask yourself what do I think about this area? What do you notice? How do you feel? What words come to your mind? These responses reflect your current way of thinking. It relates to the work you have been doing because you can control and create the way you want to think by shifting how you think.

1. Explain *mind-set* in your own words.

2. Explain *mind-shift* in your own words.

3. What mind-set would you like to shift in the dimension that you chose? Why? What are the current results that the mind-set is producing?

Activity: Mind-set and Mind-shift

15 minutes

In the dimension of wellness that you would like to improve, what is your current mind-set? What mind-shift would you like to make within the dimension of wellness? To facilitate this, I want you to identify a mind-set that may no longer be serving you and then to determine what mind-shift for you would be more beneficial.

Review: Chapters 1–6

Use these questions to review and reflect on the terms and explanations that have been shared so far.

1. What information has stood out to you? How can you use or apply the information you have received from this workbook so far?

2. What new awareness or understanding do you have now?

3. Which of the eight dimensions of wellness are you going to change right now? Why did you choose this dimension?

4. What is your current self-image of wellness in this dimension? What is your desired self-image of wellness in this dimension?

5. What are your internal and external motivations to accomplish this?

6. What is your current mind-set in this dimension? What mind-shift must occur to achieve your desired level of wellness in this dimension?

Dr. Robert L. Wilson Jr., DSL

7. What are you willing to do to improve your wellness in this dimension in reference to using the self-determination theory? What is your level of motivation? How determined are you?

8. What do you see, feel, or hear in your new desired self-image within this dimension of wellness?

7

The Power of Words

The words we use play an important role in making choices and creating wellness. Words are how you can strategically change your lifestyle, identify barriers, and create your wellness goals (Arloski 2014, 79). The way you talk about yourself and the questions you ask yourself will affect how you feel. Saying words with feeling and hearing them with your emotions reinforces your self-image, the identity that will manifest in the outcomes and results you achieve. Words without emotion will not have the strength or force to manifest the level of wellness you desire (Wilson 2023, 29).

In the next three chapters, you will be learning to identify and use your motivation to create wellness intentionally and strategically through affirmations and afformations within the dimension you're exploring. An *affirmation* tells your mind what you want, and an *afformation* allows your mind to reinforce what you want. An affirmation is a positive statement, while an afformation is a positive question to help your "inner computer" search for answers to positively reinforce the questions posed. Affirmations and afformations can be used individually or together as tools for applying the self-determination theory for yourself. The stronger the feelings and emotions connected to the affirmations and afformations, the more quickly the desired results will be produced.

This chapter and the following two will expand on the concept of self-image by bringing awareness and understanding to the words that reinforce your image of wellness as you perceive it. Your words help to describe and fortify your image. We will focus on adding value and worth to the words you speak about yourself.

For example, when I started speaking about improving my occupational wellness I was only speaking locally. I began to think about what it would be like to be a national speaker. I got into the image of being a national speaker by speaking and connecting to the feeling of traveling and speaking at different engagements, and how great it would feel to have that experience to travel nationally. That was years ago before I became a national speaker and trainer, and now I am speaking about being an international speaker and trainer. So, take full advantage of creating opportunities by speaking about what you want to be, do, and have. How will it feel once it has happened? The key is to capture the feeling now before it actually happens.

Affirmations help you build your self-image of wellness intentionally through positive programming. Afformations ask questions in a positive way to engage your mind in providing reasons to support the statement. This means that when you create an affirmation (statement), it's good to create a corresponding afformation (question) that prompts further exploration of the positive image. This internal dialogue supports and programs your behaviors to uphold and carry out the wellness image that you want. Wellness behaviors reflect your self-image of wellness.

Following are some conceptual building blocks for creating affirmations. What does each of the following descriptive terms mean to you right now?

1. positive

2. present

3. consistent

4. seen

5. heard

6. felt

In this chapter and chapters 8–9, you will be creating and working with your own affirmations and afformations. Use the following questions to align and check that your affirmations and afformations are effective for you.

1. Are they **positive**?
2. Are they in the **present** tense? (*I am,* not *I was,* or *I will be.*)
3. Are they **consistent** with the image or level of wellness that you want?
4. What do they help you to **see**? Do they help you visualize or help you to see your desired self-image?
5. What do they help you to **hear**? Do they help you locate sounds that connect you to your desired self-image?
6. What do they help you **feel?** Do they help you experience the feelings you would have in connecting to being your desired self-image?

Words can create images, feelings, and emotions that will support the external manifestation of your self-image. Using affirmations and afformations to create feelings and emotions helps you see your desired outcome now and the sensory experiences and emotions that you would have when that outcome is accomplished.

Activity: The Power of Words

15 minutes

For this activity, you get a chance to play with the possibilities. Have fun with the possibilities of who you can be, what you can do, and what you can have! Get into the details and be very descriptive. Get into the feeling of being, doing, and having your desire fulfilled.

A key component is to put your intention in the present tense ("I am") and not

Dr. Robert L. Wilson Jr., DSL

postpone it to the future ("I will"). The opportunities to create the life and wellness you want are endless and limitless, but they must be seized in the "now." How do you want to live right now? You decide. If only you can imagine and believe that it is possible, it will be yours!

Begin by creating three affirmation/afformation pairs that connect your self-image, feelings, and behavior within the wellness dimension you've chosen to explore. Let's say you've chosen the environmental dimension. An affirmation might be "I am enjoying a peaceful and pleasant environment"; the corresponding afformation could be "How am I enjoying a peaceful and pleasant environment?" Affirmations declare what is yours or what you want to attract as yours, and afformations reinforce that declaration by using your reasoning to explore what you want and why.

	Affirmation	**Afformation**
1.		
2.		
3.		

8

Affirmations

What you hear and speak will become your reality (Gomas 2017, 17). Affirmations, or intentional words, are spoken to positively influence your reality. What are you saying about yourself and your wellness? Silence your inner negative voice. Affirmations are powerful, positive, present-tense statements for empowerment. They build your mind-set and belief system to embrace the new or desired perspective. Consistently spoken affirmations with positive emotions like excitement or gratitude make an emotional connection to create images and paradigms, programming or reprogramming the way you think.

Affirmations are more than confessions of something desired or something you think would be nice to have happened. They are declarations of power, faith, and direction to feed your self-image, create feelings, and program behaviors toward your wellness goals and plans. Developing your own affirmations will help you capture the level and image of wellness you desire (Arloski 2014, 157).

1. How would you define *affirmations* in your own words?

2. How can you use affirmations to feel empowered and build your mind-set for the new perspective you desire?

3. I would like to create affirmations to help me …

Dr. Robert L. Wilson Jr., DSL

a.

b.

c.

Activity: Affirmations

15 minutes

Create three affirmations within the dimension of wellness you chose to explore and improve. What do you want to see, hear, and feel? What action can you take for each?

1. I see …

2. I hear …

3. I feel …

9

Afformations

While affirmations are positive present-tense statements that declare what you want, afformations are positive present-tense *questions* used to engage your mind to search for answers. An afformation is a powerful question with a positive spin—it provides ways to use and access your brain capacity, mental functions, and faculties in searching for an answer that reinforces what you desire from the perspective of outcomes.

Afformations allow you to develop your mind-set and belief system, providing insight and strategies that unlock an understanding of *why* we should embrace the new or desired perspective from within. If you have affirmed "I am successful," your afformation might be "Why am I so successful?" The question provides validation of the desires and goals you want to manifest and produce in your life. What makes me healthy? What makes me great at my job?

An afformation will allow you to use your mental capabilities to arrive at solutions in ways that you may not be aware of consciously. Strategically asking powerful questions will guide the process for gaining insight and answers, allowing you to shift wellness images dimensionally and assisting with changing behaviors and outcomes.

The function of an afformation is like using the internet to search for answers to a question. You are using your internal internet to search for answers to support and provide solutions for the questions you are asking. Afformations help you create an image of wellness by talking through questions and filling in details to describe your wellness image (Arloski 2014, 158).

1. How would you define *afformations* in your own words?

2. How can you use afformations to feel empowered and build your mind-set for the new perspective you desire?

3. My afformations will help me explore ... These afformations will help me explore the affirmations I created in chapter 8

   a.

   b.

   c.

Activity: Afformations

15 minutes

Write three afformations pertaining to the dimension of wellness that you would like to improve. Remember, express your afformation in the form of a question. What do you want to see, hear, and feel? What question can you create for each?

Look at the three affirmations you created for the activity in chapter 8 and create an afformation for each.

1.

2.

3.

Dr. Robert L. Wilson Jr., DSL

10

Setting SMART Goals

In part 1, you have examined your current wellness and are ready to apply the concepts presented in this workbook in order to:

- understand wellness from a dimensional and holistic perspective;
- define the role of self-awareness and self-determination in wellness;
- identify how to use self-determination theory to enhance motivation to create and increase wellness;
- define the role of self-image and feelings concerning wellness.

To succeed in implementing the information in this book, you'll need a strategic plan. A strategic plan will help you intentionally formulate your actions for your wellness plan. Start by setting goals that are:

Specific

Measurable

Achievable

Relevant

Time-oriented

Use the SMART acronym to help you tailor your goals strategically and intentionally. SMART goals will help you to be more specific in measuring or knowing how to achieve the goal and focus on ensuring that the goal is relevant and can be achieved within the time frame you want to set. When planning your desired wellness outcomes for each dimension of wellness, ask yourself the following action questions about the goal you are setting.

1. Is it **specific**? What are you going to do?
2. Is it **measurable**? How will you measure success in achieving this goal?
3. Is it **achievable**? Is your goal realistic and doable?
4. Is it **relevant** to what you want, or only what you think you can have?
5. Is it **time-oriented**? How long do you expect it will take to achieve this goal?

Activity: Setting SMART Goals

30 minutes

Create SMART goals to develop a wellness plan for the dimension of wellness you chose to explore. Use the following questions to develop a strategic plan.

1. What is your current self-image in this dimension of wellness? What self-image do you want to have?

2. What is your internal motivation?

3. What is your external motivation?

4. What is your current mind-set? What mind-shift do you need to make?

Dr. Robert L. Wilson Jr., DSL

5. Now determine whether your goal is SMART by working through the five action questions.

What **specific** actions will you take?

How will you **measure** improvement or progress?

How will you know when you **achieve** your goal?

How is the goal **relevant** to the dimension of wellness you're exploring?

How much **time** do you expect to spend reaching this goal?

11

Your Eight-Dimensional Wellness Plan

Now that you know how to develop SMART goals, use your answers to the previous action questions to write out your wellness plan. First, let's review part 1.

1. What is your definition of wellness now that you are about to complete part 1?

2. What is the connection between affirmations and afformations and your self-image, feelings, and behavior? Describe in your own words.

3. Now add what you see, how you feel, and the behavior you want to act on, using the affirmations and afformations that you previously wrote for the dimension that you chose.

Dr. Robert L. Wilson Jr., DSL

Activity: Wellness Plan

30 minutes

Use the following questions to help you develop a wellness plan for the dimension of wellness you have identified.

1. What "new" awareness do you have?

2. What is your autonomy? What is your competence? What is your relatedness?

3. What is your current mind-set? What mind-shift do you need to make to accomplish your goals?

4. What are your affirmations? What are your afformations?

5. How will your affirmations and afformations affect what you see, what you hear, and how you feel when you have accomplished your desired wellness goal?

My Wellness Plan

This page provides you with additional space to summarize and write down your SMART goals and wellness plan. Be very clear and detailed about what you will be, do, and have in your wellness plan.

Dr. Robert L. Wilson Jr., DSL

Your Strategic Goals: The "Eight Dimensions of Wellness" Plan

What's the takeaway for you? You can learn to create wellness. There are several components that will assist you in the creation process. Your motivation comes from knowing how to use your autonomy (choices), build your competence (abilities), and relate (connect) all components of success to create the wellness you desire. You have also learned to create a self-image by defining and using affirmations and afformations. Look at how far you have come. You have:

- discussed the importance and new awareness of your self-image;
- explained and identified autonomy, competence, and relatedness within the theory and practice of self-determination;
- recognized and identified your mind-set and how to make a mind-shift;
- defined affirmations and afformations;
- strategically implemented affirmations and afformations in creating wellness.

You can use this workbook to work through each of the eight dimensions of wellness, repeating the exercises. Use the following pages to identify and define your desired wellness and log your progress in each dimension.

Dimension 1: Spiritual Wellness

What is your desired self-image in the dimension of spiritual wellness?

What do you want to be? What do you want to do? What do you want to have?

How have you become more self-aware in the spiritual dimension?

How have your internal and external motivations come together to create self-motivation in the spiritual dimension?

How have you improved your autonomy, competence, and relatedness in the spiritual dimension?

What spiritual mind-set have you identified, and what mind-shift have you been acting on?

List your affirmations and afformations in the spiritual dimension. Are they positive? Are they in the present tense? Are they consistent with the image or level of wellness that you want?

What do your affirmations and afformations help you see, hear, and feel?

What spiritual goals have you been working on? What is your daily inspired practice in the spiritual dimension?

How will the spiritual dimension improve your overall wellness as you move forward?

What specific actions will you take?

How will you measure improvement or progress?

How will you know when you achieve your goal?

How is the goal relevant to the dimension of wellness you're exploring?

How much time do you expect to spend reaching this goal?

Dimension 2: Intellectual Wellness

What is your desired self-image in the dimension of intellectual wellness?

What do you want to be? What do you want to do? What do you want to have?

How have you become more self-aware in the intellectual dimension?

How have your internal and external motivations come together to create self-motivation in the intellectual dimension?

How have you improved your autonomy, competence, and relatedness in the intellectual dimension?

What intellectual mind-set have you identified, and what mind-shift have you been acting on?

List your affirmations and afformations in the intellectual dimension. Are they positive? Are they in the present tense? Are they consistent with the image or level of wellness that you want?

What do your affirmations and afformations help you see, hear, and feel?

What intellectual goals have you been working on? What is your daily inspired practice in the intellectual dimension?

How will the intellectual dimension improve your overall wellness as you move forward?

Dr. Robert L. Wilson Jr., DSL

Intellectual SMART Goals

What specific actions will you take?

How will you measure improvement or progress?

How will you know when you achieve your goal?

How is the goal relevant to the dimension of wellness you're exploring?

How much time do you expect to spend reaching this goal?

Dimension 3: Emotional Wellness

What is your desired self-image in the dimension of emotional wellness?

What do you want to be? What do you want to do? What do you want to have?

How have you become more self-aware in the emotional dimension?

How have your internal and external motivations come together to create self-motivation in the emotional dimension?

How have you improved your autonomy, competence, and relatedness in the emotional dimension?

What emotional mind-set have you identified, and what mind-shift have you been acting on?

List your affirmations and afformations in the emotional dimension. Are they positive? Are they in the present tense? Are they consistent with the image or level of wellness that you want?

Dr. Robert L. Wilson Jr., DSL

What do your affirmations and afformations help you see, hear, and feel?

What emotional goals have you been working on? What is your daily inspired practice in the emotional dimension?

How will the emotional dimension improve your overall wellness as you move forward?

Emotional SMART Goals

What specific actions will you take?

How will you measure improvement or progress?

How will you know when you achieve your goal?

How is the goal relevant to the dimension of wellness you're exploring?

How much time do you expect to spend reaching this goal?

Dimension 4: Financial Wellness

What is your desired self-image in the dimension of financial wellness?

What do you want to be? What do you want to do? What do you want to have?

How have you become more self-aware in the financial dimension?

How have your internal and external motivations come together to create self-motivation in the financial dimension?

How have you improved your autonomy, competence, and relatedness in the financial dimension?

What financial mind-set have you identified, and what mind-shift have you been acting on?

List your affirmations and afformations in the financial dimension. Are they positive? Are they in the present tense? Are they consistent with the image or level of wellness that you want?

What do your affirmations and afformations help you see, hear, and feel?

What financial goals have you been working on? What is your daily inspired practice in the financial dimension?

How will the financial dimension improve your overall wellness as you move forward?

Financial SMART Goals

What specific actions will you take?

How will you measure improvement or progress?

How will you know when you achieve your goal?

How is the goal relevant to the dimension of wellness you're exploring?

How much time do you expect to spend reaching this goal?

Dimension 5: Physical Wellness

What is your desired self-image in the dimension of physical wellness?

What do you want to be? What do you want to do? What do you want to have?

How have you become more self-aware in the physical dimension?

How have your internal and external motivations come together to create self-motivation in the physical dimension?

How have you improved your autonomy, competence, and relatedness in the physical dimension?

What physical mind-set have you identified, and what mind-shift have you been acting on?

List your affirmations and afformations in the physical dimension. Are they positive? Are they in the present tense? Are they consistent with the image or level of wellness that you want?

Dr. Robert L. Wilson Jr., DSL

What do your affirmations and afformations help you see, hear, and feel?

What physical goals have you been working on? What is your daily inspired practice in the physical dimension?

How will the physical dimension improve your overall wellness as you move forward?

Physical SMART Goals

What specific actions will you take?

How will you measure improvement or progress?

How will you know when you achieve your goal?

How is the goal relevant to the dimension of wellness you're exploring?

How much time do you expect to spend reaching this goal?

Dr. Robert L. Wilson Jr., DSL

Dimension 6: Social Wellness

What is your desired self-image in the dimension of social wellness?

What do you want to be? What do you want to do? What do you want to have?

How have you become more self-aware in the social dimension?

How have your internal and external motivations come together to create self-motivation in the social dimension?

How have you improved your autonomy, competence, and relatedness in the social dimension?

What social mind-set have you identified, and what mind-shift have you been acting on?

List your affirmations and afformations in the social dimension. Are they positive? Are they in the present tense? Are they consistent with the image or level of wellness that you want?

What do your affirmations and afformations help you see, hear, and feel?

What social goals have you been working on? What is your daily inspired practice in the social dimension?

How will the social dimension improve your overall wellness as you move forward?

Dr. Robert L. Wilson Jr., DSL

Social SMART Goals

What specific actions will you take?

How will you measure improvement or progress?

How will you know when you achieve your goal?

How is the goal relevant to the dimension of wellness you're exploring?

How much time do you expect to spend reaching this goal?

Dimension 7: Occupational Wellness

What is your desired self-image in the dimension of occupational wellness?

What do you want to be? What do you want to do? What do you want to have?

How have you become more self-aware in the occupational dimension?

How have your internal and external motivations come together to create self-motivation in the occupational dimension?

How have you improved your autonomy, competence, and relatedness in the occupational dimension?

What occupational mind-set have you identified, and what mind-shift have you been acting on?

List your affirmations and afformations in the occupational dimension. Are they positive? Are they in the present tense? Are they consistent with the image or level of wellness that you want?

Dr. Robert L. Wilson Jr., DSL

What do your affirmations and afformations help you see, hear, and feel?

What occupational goals have you been working on? What is your daily inspired practice in the occupational dimension?

How will the occupational dimension improve your overall wellness as you move forward?

Occupational SMART Goals

What specific actions will you take?

How will you measure improvement or progress?

How will you know when you achieve your goal?

How is the goal relevant to the dimension of wellness you're exploring?

How much time do you expect to spend reaching this goal?

Dr. Robert L. Wilson Jr., DSL

Dimension 8: Environmental Wellness

What is your desired self-image in the dimension of environmental wellness?

What do you want to be? What do you want to do? What do you want to have?

How have you become more self-aware in the environmental dimension?

How have your internal and external motivations come together to create self-motivation in the environmental dimension?

How have you improved your autonomy, competence, and relatedness in the environmental dimension?

What environmental mind-set have you identified, and what mind-shift have you been acting on?

List your affirmations and afformations in the environmental dimension. Are they positive? Are they in the present tense? Are they consistent with the image or level of wellness that you want?

What do your affirmations and afformations help you see, hear, and feel?

What environmental goals have you been working on? What is your daily inspired practice in the environmental dimension?

How will the environmental dimension improve your overall wellness as you move forward?

Environmental SMART Goals

What specific actions will you take?

How will you measure improvement or progress?

How will you know when you achieve your goal?

How is the goal relevant to the dimension of wellness you're exploring?

How much time do you expect to spend reaching this goal?

PART 2

Wellness Creation Journal

Introduction

The wellness journal is designed to help you put the things you learned and worked on during part 1 into your daily practice. Part 2 will help you anchor, reinforce, and reflect on how this information can assist you along your wellness creation journey.

Journaling will help raise your awareness and expand your capacity to access and create a higher level of life and wellness than you have envisioned (Dyer 2012, 25). Many workbooks help you do the work. A missing piece of the puzzle is the processing and digesting of what you worked to do. Together, the workbook and journal bridge the gap between the work and practicing the content for deeper insight and reflection. The journal will guide you in processing the information in an intentional, strategic, and powerful way that allows you the opportunity and space to be present with the process and recognize the power within you to create wellness.

So now it's time to take inspired action and create wellness for yourself. Inspired action means taking your new awareness and insights learned from this workbook, and strategically and intentionally setting goals to implement into your daily practices and lifestyle. True change starts with changing how you see your self-image, how you use affirmations and afformations to talk about your wellness and life consistently, setting and implementing your SMART goals, and taking time to reflect. Inspired action is what you can do now!

Wellness creation is about taking action from the inside out. This thirty-day journal will help you raise your awareness of how the strategic plan in part 1 works for you. The journal is structured to have you observe your perceptions of how you are experiencing the eight dimensions and describe them.

Use the space provided every day for the next thirty days to describe in detail what one or each of the eight dimensions of wellness looks, feels, and sounds like to you. You decide. Reflect, become aware, notice without judgment, with curiosity, and being present.

This is also an opportunity for you to integrate the SMART goals and wellness plan that you created for any of the eight dimensions into your observations daily over the next thirty days.

Day 1

Spiritual

Intellectual

Emotional

Financial

Physical

Social

Occupational

Environmental

Dr. Robert L. Wilson Jr., DSL

Day 2

Spiritual

Intellectual

Emotional

Financial

Physical

Social

Occupational

Environmental

Day 3

Spiritual

Intellectual

Emotional

Financial

Physical

Social

Occupational

Environmental

Dr. Robert L. Wilson Jr., DSL

Day 4

Spiritual

Intellectual

Emotional

Financial

Physical

Social

Occupational

Environmental

Day 5

Spiritual

Intellectual

Emotional

Financial

Physical

Social

Occupational

Environmental

Dr. Robert L. Wilson Jr., DSL

Day 6

Spiritual

Intellectual

Emotional

Financial

Physical

Social

Occupational

Environmental

Day 7

Spiritual

Intellectual

Emotional

Financial

Physical

Social

Occupational

Environmental

Day 8

Spiritual

Intellectual

Emotional

Financial

Physical

Social

Occupational

Environmental

Day 9

Spiritual

Intellectual

Emotional

Financial

Physical

.

Social

Occupational

Environmental

Dr. Robert L. Wilson Jr., DSL

Day 10

Spiritual

Intellectual

Emotional

Financial

Physical

Social

Occupational

Environmental

Day 11

Spiritual

Intellectual

Emotional

Financial

Physical

Social

Occupational

Environmental

Dr. Robert L. Wilson Jr., DSL

Day 12

Spiritual

Intellectual

Emotional

Financial

Physical

Social

Occupational

Environmental

Day 13

Spiritual

Intellectual

Emotional

Financial

Physical

Social

Occupational

Environmental

Dr. Robert L. Wilson Jr., DSL

Day 14

Spiritual

Intellectual

Emotional

Financial

Physical

Social

Occupational

Environmental

Day 15

Spiritual

Intellectual

Emotional

Financial

Physical

Social

Occupational

Environmental

Day 16

Spiritual

Intellectual

Emotional

Financial

Physical

Social

Occupational

Environmental

Day 17

Spiritual

Intellectual

Emotional

Financial

Physical

Social

Occupational

Environmental

Dr. Robert L. Wilson Jr., DSL

Day 18

Spiritual

Intellectual

Emotional

Financial

Physical

Social

Occupational

Environmental

Day 19

Spiritual

Intellectual

Emotional

Financial

Physical

Social

Occupational

Environmental

Dr. Robert L. Wilson Jr., DSL

Day 20

Spiritual

Intellectual

Emotional

Financial

Physical

Social

Occupational

Environmental

Day 21

Spiritual

Intellectual

Emotional

Financial

Physical

Social

Occupational

Environmental

Dr. Robert L. Wilson Jr., DSL

Day 22

Spiritual

Intellectual

Emotional

Financial

Physical

Social

Occupational

Environmental

Day 23

Spiritual

Intellectual

Emotional

Financial

Physical

Social

Occupational

Environmental

Dr. Robert L. Wilson Jr., DSL

Day 24

Spiritual

Intellectual

Emotional

Financial

Physical

Social

Occupational

Environmental

Day 25

Spiritual

Intellectual

Emotional

Financial

Physical

Social

Occupational

Environmental

Dr. Robert L. Wilson Jr., DSL

Day 26

Spiritual

Intellectual

Emotional

Financial

Physical

Social

Occupational

Environmental

Day 27

Spiritual

Intellectual

Emotional

Financial

Physical

Social

Occupational

Environmental

Dr. Robert L. Wilson Jr., DSL

Day 28

Spiritual

Intellectual

Emotional

Financial

Physical

Social

Occupational

Environmental

Day 29

Spiritual

Intellectual

Emotional

Financial

Physical

Social

Occupational

Environmental

 Dr. Robert L. Wilson Jr., DSL

Day 30

Spiritual

Intellectual

Emotional

Financial

Physical

Social

Occupational

Environmental

Progress and Results Tracker

The progress and results tracker is a tool to aid you in noticing and becoming more aware of your progress and power to create results during this journey. Notice your new awareness and insight regarding your challenges, opportunities, resources, progress, and results. How will you use the information you have gained to advance your wellness goals going forward? What will that look, feel, or sound like for you?

To help you track and summarize your progress and results, ask yourself the following questions and record your answers after the thirty days.

- What are my challenges?
- What are your opportunities?
- What are my resources?
- What progress have I made?
- What are my results?

Thirty-Day Reflections

During your thirty-day journey, what self-discovery did you notice?

During your thirty-day journey, what self-education did you notice?

During your thirty-day journey, what self-motivation did you notice?

What did you learn about your self-determination and motivation in creating your wellness plan?

What mind-set has changed, and what new beliefs have become part of your mind-shift?

Which of the affirmations and afformations that you created were most useful in guiding your wellness journey?

What new wellness self-image did the tools in this workbook help you create?

How will you apply what you learned through this process to create your next wellness goals or plans?

Taking Inspired Action

Now that you have completed the thirty-day journey, what are your next steps? How will you use the information and concepts in this workbook to help you? How has using the journal helped you? How will you apply and incorporate the information, skills, and tools provided by this workbook and journal into your life and practices moving forward?

Thank you for allowing me to be your guide along this amazing
and transformative journey that you decided to embark on.
Continued success in creating the wellness and life you want and deserve!

References

Books and Journals

Arloski, M. (2014). *Wellness Coaching for Lasting Lifestyle Change*, 2nd ed. Duluth, MN: Whole Person Associates.

Dyer, W. W. (1997). *Manifest Your Destiny: The Nine Spiritual Principles for Getting Everything You Want*. New York, NY: Harper Collins.

Dyer, W. W. (2012). *Wishes Fulfilled: Mastering the Art of Manifesting*. New York, NY: Hay House.

Gomas, D. C. (2017). *Christian Life Coaching Bible*. www.dennisgomas.com.

Hajian, Shiva. 2019. "Transfer of Learning and Teaching: A Review of Transfer Theories and Effective Instructional Practices." *IAFOR Journal of Education* 7 (1): 93–111.

Hill, N. (2017). *How to Own Your Own Mind*. New York, NY: Penguin Random House.

Martela, F. and Ryan, R.M. (2015). "The Benefits of Benevolence: Basic Psychological Needs, Beneficence, and the Enhancement of Well-Being." *Journal of Personality* 84: 1–15.

Proctor, Bob. (2021). *Change Your Paradigm, Change Your Life: Flip That Switch Now!* Middletown, DE: G&D Media.

Ryan, R. M., and Deci, E. L. (2020). "Intrinsic and Extrinsic Motivation from a Self-Determination Theory Perspective: Definitions, Theory, Practices, and Future Directions." *Contemporary Educational Psychology* 61 (April), 101860.

Schneider, B. (2022). *The 7 Level Framework for Mastery in Life and Business: Energy Leadership*, 2nd ed. Hoboken, NJ: John Wiley & Sons.

Wilson Jr., R. L. (2023). *Self-Image: Your Vision of Wellness*. Bloomington, IN: Archway Publishing.

Wilson Jr., R. L. (2023). *Words That Create Wellness: Using Affirmations and Afformations*. Bloomington, IN: Archway Publishing.

WEBSITES

The Center for Self-Determination Theory (CSDT), https://selfdeterminationtheory.org.

INLP Center, https://inlpcenter.org/actp-coach-training-for-pcc-icf.

National Wellness Institute, https://nationalwellness.org.

SAMHSA's Wellness Initiative, https://store.samhsa.gov/product/SAMHSA-s-Wellness-Initiative-Wellness-Community-Power-Point-Presentation/sma16-4955.

About the Author

 Dr. Robert L. Wilson Jr., DSL is an author, entrepreneur, consultant, speaker, coach, and trainer. He has a doctorate in strategic leadership with a concentration in global consulting from Regent University. He received a master's degree in sociology from Fayetteville State University and a bachelor's in psychology from Rowan University. He is a Certified Professional Life Coach (CPLC), Certified Wellness Coach (CWC), Certified Life Coach (CLC), Certified Practitioner of Neuro-Linguistic Programming (P-NLP), Certified Master Practitioner of Neuro-Linguistic Programming (M-NLP), Certified Mindfulness Practitioner, Certified Practitioner of Hypnosis, and a Certified Hypnotherapist.

Dr. Wilson is the owner and principal consultant of Robert Wilson Consulting and Wilson Global Outreach Solutions LLC, as well as, the founder and lead trainer of Global Solutions Education and Training Academy. He has worked in the field of mental health, leadership, and organizational development for more than twenty years. His areas of focus are personal, professional, leadership, and organizational education, development, and training. He is a National Trainer and Certified Mental Health First Aid Instructor for the adult and youth curriculum.

Other books by Dr. Robert L. Wilson Jr., DSL

Self-Image: Your Vision of Wellness
Words That Create Wellness: Using Affirmations and Afformations

Global Solutions Education and Training Academy
Online Courses and Subscriptions

Conflict Resolution: Building Effective Communication
Skills from the Inside Out
Shifting Your Energy for Success
Leadership: Leading from a Wellness Perspective
Relaxation: Developing Ways to Effectively Reduce and Manage Stress
Wellness and Resilience: Building Inner Resources
Wellness Creation
Organizational Wellness: Creating a Wellness Culture

Subscriptions available at the VIP, Platinum, Gold, and Silver levels

For additional information about products, programs, or services please contact:

Dr. Robert L. Wilson Jr., DSL, CPLC, CWC
Owner and Principal Consultant
Robert Wilson Consulting
Wilson Global Outreach Solutions LLC
www.WilsonGOS.com
Robert@WilsonGOS.com

Global Solutions Education and Training Academy
https://globalsolutionseducationandtrainingacademy.learnworlds.com

Printed in the United States
by Baker & Taylor Publisher Services